GRACE
HOPPER

PROGRAMMING PIONEER

GRACE HOPPER

PROGRAMMING PIONEER

BY NANCY WHITELAW

ILLUSTRATED BY JANET HAMLIN

Scientific American

BOOKS FOR YOUNG READERS

W. H. FREEMAN AND COMPANY ◆ NEW YORK

For Gordon Smith and Winifred Asprey

Acknowledgments

Many people answered my queries for information on Grace Hopper. To all of them she was Amazing Grace, and they were eager to participate in a book that celebrated Admiral Hopper's life and work.

They are, in alphabetical order: Jim Adams, Dr. Winifred Asprey, Jill Baylor, Richard Bloch, Admiral Peter Cullins, Vassar College Historian Elizabeth Daniels, Mabel Davies, Jean Davis, Rosetta Desrosiers, Anne Drummond, J. Presper Eckert, Eileen Fischer, Jane Gefvert, Bernice George, Judith Hanna, Virginia Henckel, Marie Kelleher, Sylvia Kessler, Mary Leiper, Mike Maynard, Jim McGarvey, Judy Moss, Roger Murray, Acting Secretary of the Nacy Sean O'Keefe, Anne O'Neill, Constance Rawson, Jim Senior, Jonah Sherman, Gordon Smith, Radcliffe College Librarian Wendy Thomas, Professor Henry Tropp, Mary Westcote, Harry Wulforst, Rita Yavinsky.

I want to give special thanks to Dr. Alice Fischer, author of *The Anatomy of Programming Languages,* for her skill and patience in reviewing the manuscript.

—*N. W.*

Text copyright © 1995 by Nancy Whitelaw.

Illustrations copyright © by Janet Hamlin.

All rights reserved.

Scientific American Books for Young Readers is an imprint of
W. H. Freeman and Company, 41 Madison Avenue,
New York, NY 10010

Library of Congress Cataloging-in-Publication Data

Whitelaw, Nancy.

Grace Hopper: programming pioneer/by Nancy Whitelaw; illustrated by Janet Hamlin.

(Science Superstars)

Includes index.

Summary: Presents the life and career of the admiral who was also "the grandmother of the computer age."

ISBN 0-7167-6598-5 (hardcover).—ISBN 0-7167-6599-3 (softcover).

1. Hopper, Grace Murray—Juvenile literature. 2. United States. Navy—Officers—Biography—Juvenile literature. 3. United States. Navy—Women—Biography—Juvenile literature. 4. Admirals—United States Navy—Biography. 5. Women computer programmers—United States—Biography—Juvenile literature. 6. Computer engineers—United States—Biography—Juvenile literature. [1. Hopper, Grace Murray. 2. Admirals. 3. Computer engineers. 4. Women—Biography]

I. Hamlin, Janet, ill. II. Title. III. Series.

V63.H66W49 1995   004'.092—dc20   [B]   95-18690   CIP   AC

Printed in the United States of America.

10 9 8 7 6 5 4 3 2 1

CONTENTS

Introduction

Have you ever wondered what it would be like to be famous? What if you invented something important or discovered something no one else knew about? What if people called you great or brilliant or brave?

I wonder about it a lot. That's one of the reasons I write biographies. I like learning about famous people.

This is what I learned about Grace Murray Hopper when I first began to study her life:

- She had a happy childhood.
- She graduated with honors from one of the best colleges in the country.
- When she taught, her students admired her.
- When she programmed software, the people she worked with called her a genius.
- The United States Navy made her a rear admiral—the second female rear admiral in history.

I became fascinated with this woman who seemed to have had no difficulties in life. I had lots of questions. Some of them were:

- When Grace was a child, did she know what she wanted to be when she grew up?
- How did she come up with her ideas?

- Did she ever have problems?
- Did everybody—really everybody—admire her?
- Was she smarter than most people or harder-working or luckier?
- What did she do for fun?
- Who were her heroes?

I wanted to find answers to these questions, so I became a detective. A good way to start finding out about a person is to talk with that person. I couldn't talk with Grace Hopper. She had died in 1992. So I read everything I could find written about her—books, articles in computer journals and other magazines, and newspaper write-ups. I read articles and speeches she had written herself. I talked with her family, friends, and co-workers. I found answers to some of my questions, but not all.

Then I began writing. I put together facts, ideas, and answers, and a few more questions. This is what I found out about how Grace Hopper reached her goals. It is the story of a woman who was often called "Amazing Grace."

CHAPTER 1

Growing Up Curious

Seven-year-old Grace Murray was curious. She had to know what made her wind-up clock ring like crazy. All day the round-faced clock sat ticking away peacefully. Every morning it screeched as loudly as a train whistle until she got up and shut it off.

One day Grace found a screwdriver and unscrewed the back plate. Gears and wheels and springs dropped onto the table. Some of the gears were the size of her thumbnail; others were bigger. Some of the tiny wheels were connected to springs. Grace didn't see anything that looked as if it could make that screeching noise.

Maybe if she put the pieces back together, she could see what made the sound. But they had dropped out so fast that she didn't know how to fit them back into the case. Luckily for her, each of the seven bedrooms in her house had an alarm clock. So she had six more chances to satisfy her curiosity.

One after another, persistent Grace opened the backs of the other six clocks. Each time, the pieces fell out before she could see how they fit together. She ended up with seven piles of gears, springs, and wheels—and seven clock cases.

If she had been a boy, people would have said, "Oh, he's on his way to becoming an engineer!" But Grace was a girl, born in 1906. In the early twentieth century, girls from well-to-do families were usually expected to become wives and mothers with no other career goals. So Grace didn't think much about what she wanted to do when she grew up.

Grace was simply fascinated with machines. If something moved back and forth or up and down or around and around, she wanted to

know how it worked. Her parents, Walter and Mary Murray, didn't mind if Grace played with machines while other girls had tea parties for their dolls. These unusual parents wanted their daughter to be able to have a career as well as to be a wife and mother.

Indoors on rainy days Grace liked to build with a collection of nuts, bolts, and construction material called a Structiron kit. She spent hours creating elevators, wagons, and other vehicles too weird to name. With a small electric motor, she made the elevators go up and down. She made her contraptions move from one place to another.

Grace's first hero was probably her mother. Mary Murray did more than care for the three children: Grace, the oldest; Mary, three years younger; and Roger, two years younger than Mary. Grace's mother took on family responsibilities that were usually handled by husbands.

She had to do this because Walter Murray suffered from a problem commonly called hardening of the arteries. His legs did not get enough blood, so they hurt and felt weak. Nowadays people with hardening of the arteries take medication that makes the blood flow more easily. These medicines weren't available in the early 1900s, so doctors amputated Walter Murray's legs. Throughout her husband's long and painful recovery, Grace's mother paid the bills, kept accounts, planned spending, and figured out tax payments. Watching her mother, Grace became fascinated with columns of numbers, with adding and subtracting, and especially with getting answers.

Grace admired her father too. He never complained about having lost his legs. He even joked as he strapped his heavy wooden legs around his knees and fastened them with thick, metal joints. "It's almost six months since I've changed my socks."

Every June, the Murrays packed their bags into their Model T Ford, left their home in New York City, and drove to Lake Wentworth in New Hampshire. The trips were three-day adventures. There were only about one hundred thousand cars in the whole country then, and few roads. The only map available was a geological survey map that showed hills, rivers, and mountains—but no roads. There were no gas stations, so Grace's family strapped gasoline in five-gallon cans onto the back of the car.

Lake Wentworth was an exciting place to spend the summer. Grace loved the family's sail-canoe, a single-sailed boat that was a little heavier than a regular canoe. Sailing was tricky on Lake Wentworth because of gusty northwest winds that changed quickly. Grace might skim along smoothly for several minutes. Then suddenly she would find herself soaked as waves broke over the sides of the canoe. Sometimes the canoe filled with water fast enough to sink it. Then Grace had to flip it upside down and swim back to shore, pulling the canoe along after her.

Capsizing a canoe was embarrassing for Grace, the great-granddaughter of Alexander Russell, who had been a rear admiral in the United States Navy. Great-grandpa Russell was Grace's biggest hero after her mother and father even though Grace had met him only once, when she was just three years old. She had thought he looked very important with his white muttonchop whiskers and silver-topped cane. Wouldn't he be ashamed to see his great-granddaughter towing a boat instead of sailing it?

Grace didn't have special friends at Lake Wentworth. She joined any group that was doing something fun. On summer evenings when the lake was calm, Grace often took a boat out to the middle of the lake with a group of kids. There they watched the sunset and sang. Sometimes Grace played the ukelele.

Grace loved to read. Her sister still has some of the books that she and Grace read over and over again, including the longtime girls' favorite *Little Women* by Louisa May Alcott. There was also a series by G. A. Henty called *The Boys' Own Library*. In these books, the heroes—all boys—traveled to faraway places seeking adventure. Grace wanted adventure too. In a time when very few people had even flown in an airplane, Grace imagined traveling to the stars.

The legends of North American Indian tribes fascinated Grace. She learned stories about Chiefs Chocuro and Kankamaugus, whose names were given to mountains near Lake Wentworth. With great drama and excitement, Grace retold these legends using puppets she had made. Mary and Roger made fun of her exaggerated actions and speech, but that didn't stop her. She loved to perform.

Every August the Murrays went back to New York City. Walter returned to his insurance business there, and the children went to private schools. Back in the city it was time for Grace to put away her bathing suits and play clothes. Her mother insisted she look like a lady in school. This meant wearing below-the-knee dresses and high-button shoes. The worst part was wearing garters to hold up cotton stockings that fit over long underwear.

For Grace, New York wasn't just school. Sometimes after school she helped her grandfather, John Van Horne, a surveyor for New York City. Part of his job was to plan new streets for the fast-growing metropolis.

Grandpa Van Horne let Grace hold his red-and-white striped surveyor's pole for him. Holding that pole straight and steady was not as easy as it looked. It was about twice as tall as Grace and as big around as a broomstick. If she let the pole wobble, Grandpa might calculate distances incorrectly. Then the streets and sidewalks he planned would

not meet at nice sharp corners. Grace watched as her grandfather recorded measurements and distances. She loved learning about angles, curves, and intersections.

Years later, when Grace talked about her childhood, she gave her family much of the credit for her success: "My mother's very great interest in mathematics and my father's, a house full of books, a constant interest in learning, an early interest in reading, and insatiable curiosity...these were a primary influence all the way along."

CHAPTER 2

Absolutely Dazzling

In third grade, Grace had some poetry published in the school yearbook. The first two lines were like many other poems of the day:

> Faithfulness in all things
> My motto is, you see;

In her last two lines, Grace showed her spunk and humor:

> The world will be a better place
> When all agree with me.

Grace's love of fun didn't keep her from working hard at school. The Murray children were expected to be the best in their classes. Often their parents rewarded them with little presents such as a ring or other piece of jewelry. When their grades were a little lower than usual, a parent would say, "You can do better." And on the next report card they always did.

Grace learned to expect that she would be at the head of her class. But she didn't become a snob because of her high marks. Being a top student was a natural part of her life.

In 1917, when Grace was ten years old, the United States entered World War I. American soldiers and sailors traveled across the Atlantic Ocean to fight in Europe.

Grace was very patriotic. Some of her ancestors were Revolutionary War heroes, and her special hero was great-grandpa Russell, the Navy admiral. But Grace did not imagine becoming a soldier or a sailor herself. American women were not allowed to join the military units, except the Nursing Corps and Reserve branches.

President Woodrow Wilson asked civilians to knit for soldiers, sailors, and marines who needed blankets, socks, and caps during the year and a half until the war ended. Grace and her classmates answered the President's call. They were proud to be involved in a patriotic assignment.

When Grace enrolled in high school, she was five feet six inches tall and weighed less than a hundred pounds. She said that she knew she wasn't pretty but that it didn't bother her much. Her mind was on her studies.

She was in high school during the Roaring Twenties, when people's lives changed in ways they had never imagined. More and more people owned automobiles, and they drove on parkways. And they were more likely to light their houses with electricity than with gas. People could buy radios, electric washing machines, and hundreds of other new inventions. Pictures were sent by television for the first time.

In 1923, when she was seventeen years old, Grace took entrance exams for Vassar College. She wanted to major in math. After graduation she thought she might become a math teacher or perhaps work in insurance like her father. But Grace had a problem—she failed the Latin section of the test.

Disappointed, but not defeated, she resolved to take the test again the next spring. In the meantime, she enrolled in Hartridge School in New Jersey, which specialized in college preparation. She studied hard—especially Latin! And in the spring, Grace passed the college entrance exam. She enrolled at Vassar in September 1924.

Vassar, a college in upstate New York, was at that time just for women. School bulletins from the 1920s give a good look at life there. Much of Vassar life was formal. In a solemn ceremony on the first day of school, members of the upper classes wore white dresses as they

greeted new students. Students always wore skirts and blouses or dresses to classes. They attended afternoon teas at the homes of their instructors. In the dining room, maids served meals, and each table was set with a white tablecloth and napkins.

Grace majored in math and physics. The two subjects fit together well because physicists use a lot of math as they study matter and energy. In a physics course she built a spectroscope, an instrument that breaks light into all its different colors. She had come a long way from building elevators with her Structiron kit.

A professor asked Grace to help a student who was failing physics. After just a few sessions, Grace realized that she enjoyed teaching. So she did more of it.

Sometimes she held tutoring sessions for several students at a time. The young lady who had acted out Native American legends brought drama to her teaching. For one lesson, she filled a bathtub half full of water. The students dropped pencils, hair brushes, and other objects into the tub. Then they "dropped in" one of the students. This experiment illustrated the theory of displacement, the fact that the water line of a container rises according to the weight of objects dropped into it.

Almost seventy years later, Mary Leiper, a fellow student, remembers Grace vividly. Mary had cut most of her classes in advanced math, so she was worried she would fail the final exam. "I was sitting at lunch, looking sadly at my plate, " she recollects. Grace came by and asked, "What's the matter?" Mary told her. Grace invited Mary to come to her room.

"In about forty-five minutes," recounts Mary, "she laid before me the complete skeleton, the philosophy of the course. What she did was absolutely dazzling." She adds happily, "I passed!"

Dazzling! Brilliant! Classmates used these words to describe Grace in the classroom. Outside of class, they said, she was a quiet student with few interests except study and research. In her senior

year, Grace was elected to Phi Beta Kappa, a national honorary society for students who earn top grades. She won a Vassar College Fellowship, which granted money for further education, and she enrolled at Yale University in New Haven, Connecticut. There she started a two-year program for a master's degree in mathematics.

The next summer, while on vacation at Lake Wentworth, she met Vincent Hopper, an English instructor at New York University. They had a lot in common. They were the same age, and they both loved learning and teaching. They began to date. Even on a date Grace was sometimes so busy thinking about math that she couldn't pay attention to Vincent. She loved to tell a story about Vincent's complaining. She quoted him: "When you date a mathematician, you plan a great romantic evening. She doesn't respond. After two hours, she says, 'I've got it! It's zero!'"

The young couple kept in touch with each other throughout the next year. Shortly after Grace earned her master's degree at Yale, she and Vincent were married.

CHAPTER 3

—wW—

"I Love the Color Blue"

In the 1930s, Americans faced an economic depression that left one out of every four workers unemployed. Grace worried about finding a job when she and Vincent returned from their European honeymoon. Although married women were not expected to work, Grace wanted to get back to her math.

She didn't worry long. "Vassar offered me a position teaching math at $800 a year, and I jumped at it."

Grace's students learned to expect the unexpected. For homework in a probability course, Grace required her students to play a card game called bridge and also to study games with dice. Questions on her exams asked students to predict results in card games and other games of chance. In another course she handed out the final exam—the big test students would take at the end of the term—on the first day. She said that left no questions about what she expected her students to learn. Another time she asked the students to write their own final exam. That showed her what they considered most important in the course.

Grace tried to show students how significant math is in everyday life. She had them invent a city by planning buildings, figuring out how much money it would cost to run the city, and how to get that money. They also learned how the city would have to change as its citizens and their needs changed. Some teachers at Vassar criticized the way Grace taught. They thought she should focus on pure math without showing how it works in the world. However, school officials recognized that Grace was communicating a love of math as well as a review of the basic skills. She was allowed to continue teaching in her special way.

Grace and Vincent built a house on the Vassar campus, with a garage for their Model A Ford. Grace's parents frequently stayed with the young couple.

Winifred Asprey, who lives in that house now, was a friend of the Hoppers. According to her, Grace and Vincent kept a box of cracked and chipped dishes just inside the kitchen door that led to the garage. Anyone in the family who was annoyed could open the kitchen door and throw a dish at the garage wall. The sound of the smash helped calm the angry person, and the broken pieces fell harmlessly into a trash can placed there for just that purpose.

Grace loved teaching, but she also loved studying. So she decided to study more math at Yale. Vincent was studying too, at Columbia University in New York City. They were so busy that sometimes they saw each other only on weekends. In 1934, Grace earned her Ph.D. degree in mathematics from Yale.

Despite her busy schedule of both teaching and learning, Grace kept up with the news of the day. By 1940 many nations, in both Europe and Asia, were at war. In December 1941, Japanese forces attacked Pearl Harbor, an American naval base in Hawaii. The United States joined Great Britain, the Soviet Union, China, and other Allies to fight against Japan, Germany, Italy, and other Axis countries in World War II.

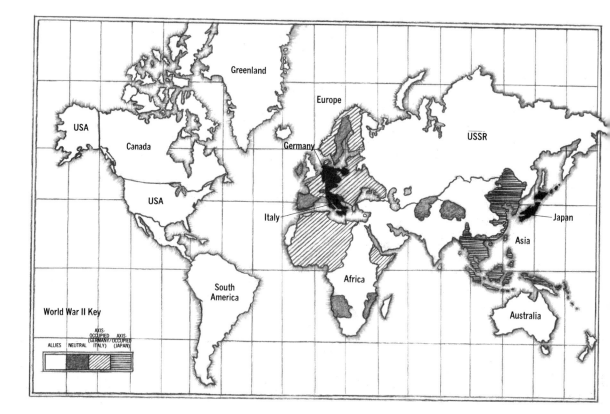

Greenland

Europe

USSR

USA

Canada

Germany

USA

Italy

Japan

Asia

South
America

Africa

Australia

World War II Key

AXIS-
OCCUPIED AXIS-
(GERMANY/ OCCUPIED
ALLIES NEUTRAL ITALY) (JAPAN)

Just as in World War I, American citizens rushed to show support for their country. More than fifteen million men volunteered or were drafted into the military. One hundred twenty thousand women wore military uniforms, serving as nurses and in office jobs as clerks, typists, and telephone operators. Across the country, ten million men and women worked on assembly lines producing airplanes, tanks, guns, and other military supplies. Everyone saved paper, rubber, tin, and aluminum for recycling, as these materials were needed for military purposes. People planted vegetable gardens—popularly called Victory Gardens—since many farmers and other food suppliers had left their jobs to serve in the military.

Grace's husband and brother both joined the Army Air Forces. Her sister worked in a General Electric plant that made devices used in bombs.

In the summer of 1942, Grace was teaching summer school at Barnard College in New York City. Every day marching sailors passed by her dormitory. "The more they went by, the more I wanted to be in the Navy also," she said. But the Navy did not accept women.

Thousands of sailors were injured and killed in Pacific Ocean battles. Soon there was a serious shortage of men who could serve. Officials decided to allow women to work in Navy offices in the United States so that men would be free to serve overseas. Congress created the WAVES—Women Accepted for Voluntary Emergency Service. A recruiting poster showed a smiling young woman in a blue-and-white uniform. The caption said: "Enlist in the WAVES—Release a Man to Fight at Sea."

Grace was eager to enlist. She made a joke out of her eagerness years later when an interviewer on the *60 Minutes* TV show asked why she joined the WAVES. She told him that she wanted to sign up "because there was a war on and everybody was going into something. I'd had a [great-] grandfather who was a rear admiral....Besides, I love the color blue."

But the Navy was not interested in her great-grandfather or her color preference. When she tried to enlist, they turned her down. They gave three reasons for rejecting her. She was 36, and that was too old. She weighed 105 pounds, and that was too light. She was a math teacher, and government officials believed that math teachers needed to stay in colleges to teach future soldiers and sailors.

Grace convinced officials that she could perform Navy duties even though she was "old" and light. But there was still the problem of her job. Since math teachers could not enlist, she took a six-month leave of absence from Vassar. Then she returned to the recruitment center, no longer a math teacher. In 1943 she was sworn in as a member of the Women's Reserve of the United States Naval Reserve.

She was assigned to Midshipman's School, a training school for officers, at Smith College in Northampton, Massachusetts. Grace and five hundred other trainees were all college graduates, used to work-

ing hard in courses. The easiest part of their schedule was classwork and studying.

The more difficult part was learning the requirements and customs of military life. The young women spent hours in calisthenics, improving their body strength, agility, and posture. They marched back and forth in rows across the campus. They even had to march in rows when they went shopping in Northampton. Every morning they tucked in their bed covers so tightly that an officer could bounce a quarter on their bedspreads. They wore their uniforms most of the time.

Grace loved military life. "I didn't even have to bother to decide what I was going to wear in the morning," she said. "I didn't have to figure out what I was going to cook for dinner. . . . I had a perfectly heavenly time."

Trainees learned to tell the difference between Allied and Axis airplanes. They learned to identify American B-17s, British Spitfires, and German Messerschmidts. They could recognize profiles of cargo ships, battleships, minesweepers, submarines, and other craft. Grace found this study particularly easy because she had spent a lot of time working with drawing and space projections in math. She graduated at the top of her class from Midshipman's School in June 1944. She was now Lieutenant JG (junior grade) Grace Murray Hopper. Her first assignment was to work with computers at Harvard University.

CHAPTER 4

—•WV•—

"The Fanciest Gadget
I'd Ever Seen"

In 1944 few people had ever heard of a computer. But the idea of a counting machine had been around for over 2,500 years. About 500 B.C., the Chinese started to use an abacus, a set of rods that held movable counters. The abacus user moved a bead for each number up to ten. Then the user moved a bead on a higher rod to indicate that a new group of ten was being counted.

The next useful counting machine was invented by French mathematician Blaise Pascal about two thousand years later. It was a set of interlocking cogs and wheels on an axle. The user "dialed" the numbers he or she wanted to add into the machine, putting the "ones" onto the farthest right wheel, the "tens" next to that, the "hundreds" next to that, and so on. When the "ones" had rotated all the way around and back to zero, the machine made the "tens" wheel move one notch forward. A number appeared in a window, indicating the position of the wheels at any given time.

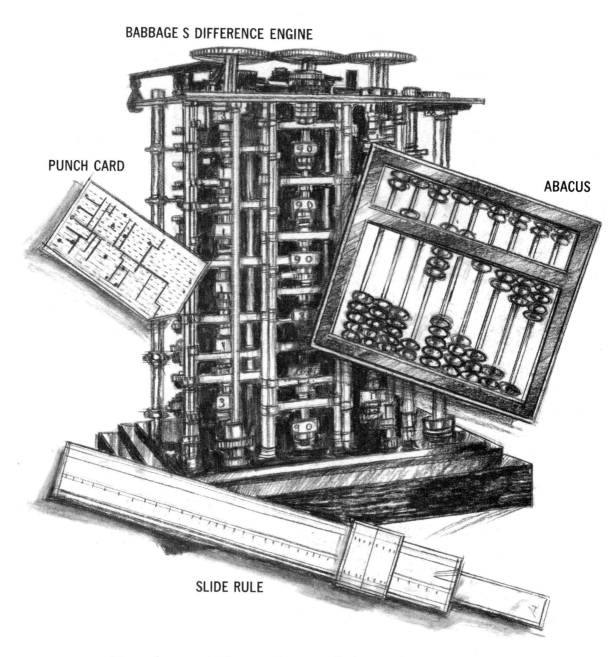

BABBAGE'S DIFFERENCE ENGINE

PUNCH CARD

ABACUS

SLIDE RULE

Nowadays a similar machine, called an odometer, measures the distance a car travels. Each time the car wheel rotates, the dial moves a little. When it has moved one mile's worth of rotations, a new figure appears in a window on the dashboard. This figure changes with each mile of wheel rotations.

Another counting machine was the slide rule, invented by William Oughtred in the early 1600s. This is a set of connected rulers imprinted with mathematical tables that can be used to do multiplication, division, and more advanced calculations. The user slides a middle "ruler" back and forth so that one end lines up with the multiplier. The answer then lies opposite the multiplicand. The user reads the answer by estimating the distance from the nearest mark on the scale. The slide rule is faster than the abacus and the mechanical calculator. But it does not give exact answers, since the scales are not detailed enough. Instead it gives an answer that is close to the correct one. A slide rule will tell you that the answer to 5,432 x 4,739 is approximately 25,700,000. The actual answer is 25,742,248.

In the early 1800s, a weaver named Joseph Jacquard contributed an idea that became useful in a counting machine. Like all weavers, he used a shuttle to carry threads through the loom. A series of tiny hooks raised some of the threads, allowing the shuttle to pass through with the desired color thread.

Jacquard thought of the idea of punching holes in cards to control the hooks. Where there was a hole, the hook passed through the card and lifted the thread. Where there was no hole, the hook was blocked, so the thread was not raised. For each row of weaving, Jacquard punched a different card.

In the late 1890s, inventor Herman Hollerith imitated this punched card idea to make the most advanced calculator up to that time. Instead of patterns, the holes in Hollerith's cards represented numbers. Rods passed through the punched holes into a bowl of mercury, creating an electrical circuit. The electricity caused wheels to turn, recording the numbers indicated by the holes in the cards. The totals appeared in open windows as they did with Pascal's machine. This was the first electromechanical counting machine, a kind of computer.

The computer that Grace Hopper worked with at Harvard was far more advanced than Hollerith's machine. The eight-foot-high

Mark I spread across the walls of a large room. Through the glass frame, Grace could see thousands of small electromechanical relay switches. Tiny round lights blinked on and off all along the length of the machine. Four glass-encased reels held rolls of paper tape to be fed into the machine. This tape recorded the computer "program," the series of instructions to be performed.

Off to one side stood the row of "typewriters" that would record information received from the computer. The machines clicked and clacked away, making Grace think of a room full of knitters.

With just one look, Grace was hooked. "It was the fanciest gadget I'd ever seen," she said. "I had to find out how it worked." "Fancy gadget" was an interesting description for this machine that weighed five tons and contained over eight hundred thousand parts connected by five hundred miles of wire.

Grace's commander, Howard Aiken, hoped that the Mark I would give soldiers the information they needed to keep up with modern weapons. Using new technologies, military researchers had created sophisticated tools of warfare: self-propelled rockets, large and complex guns, and powerful bombs.

If a gunner placed his weapon at a certain angle from the ground, he could send the bullet or shell a certain distance. If he changed the angle, the distance would change. Information in a firing table would tell him how to select the proper angle for his particular task. The firing table also displayed information on how weather conditions affected the speed and direction of a missile.

Researchers at the Ballistics Research Laboratory received orders for more than forty firing tables a week, but they could complete only fifteen. Commander Aiken asked Grace and her colleagues to program Mark I to produce these tables faster than researchers could.

Mark I had a great advantage over researchers. It could work twenty-four hours a day and never become tired or bored. It also had a couple of disadvantages. One was that it could not move from one step to the next without specific instructions each time. Another was

that it could react to only two signals—"switch ON" and "switch OFF."

Grace first identified the formulas necessary for a particular firing table. Then she rewrote each formula as a series of steps, or instructions. This rewriting was time consuming and tedious. If she were tired or bored or working too fast, she could easily make a mistake. She might write a 7 that looked like a 1 or a 4 that looked like a 9. She might skip a step or write the same step twice.

Her next task was to "translate" the formula numbers into binary code, a counting system that uses only two digits: 0 and 1. (Counting in binary goes like this: 0, 1, 10, 11, 100....)

Once Grace had the formula steps written in binary code, she had to "translate" the code into a language that Mark I could "read." This language was a series of punched holes in reels of paper tape to be fed into the computer. She punched holes to indicate 1's, and Mark I read these as commands to switch ON. She left covered the places that indicated 0's. Mark I read these as switch OFF, since the current did not flow through.

If Grace misread a numeral or skipped a line when punching in the code, Mark I would come up with the wrong answer. At that point she would have to check each step in her notes and then compare the notes to the punches in the tapes. Then she would have to start over again from the place where she had made the mistake.

In spite of all the problems, the work with Mark I was successful. Programming the computer to produce the tables took much less time than doing all the calculations by hand. Grace and seven other workers kept Mark I running twenty-four hours a day. They took turns sleeping at the office in case the computer stopped working in the middle of the night.

Grace and her team members learned how to speed the tasks of coding, translating, punching cards, and recording results. When one of them worked out a shortcut, he or she shared it with the others. This sharing saved a lot of time.

Commander Aiken wanted other computer workers to have the advantage of the shortcuts.

"You're going to write a book," he ordered Grace.

"I can't write a book," she answered.

"You're in the Navy now," Aiken replied.

That was all he needed to say. In 1946, Harvard University Press published her book, *A Manual of Operation for the Automatic Sequence Controlled Calculator.*

Grace spent more and more time in the computer lab. Years later, when an interviewer asked her about her social life, she replied, "You didn't go out in the evening and drink beer and compare notes on problems. You were dead tired and you went home and you went to bed because you were going to be there at the crack of dawn the next morning."

Grace moved ahead quickly in the field of computers. By the summer of 1945, she was working on the construction of a new computer—the Mark II. This machine was five times faster than the Mark I because it could handle more information at one time.

One hot summer evening, when Grace and her team had left the windows open, hoping to catch a breeze, Mark II suddenly stopped. Grace used her pocket mirror to check the switches behind the front panel. There she discovered a moth squashed on a switch. The insect had broken an electrical contact and had shut off the machine. Grace pulled the moth out with tweezers and taped it in the daily log book. She bragged that she had "de-bugged" the computer. Today, to "de-bug" means to solve a problem in a computer program and to get it working again. Many people say Grace created the word.

CHAPTER 5

Amazing Grace

In August 1945, when World War II ended, Grace and Vincent hadn't lived together for many years. That same year they were divorced. They had no children.

By then, Grace loved everything about the Navy—the training, her job at Harvard, military discipline, and the opportunity to serve. So she decided to stay in the WAVES. As a reservist she worked part time as a computer consultant and lecturer. Her knowledge was valuable because the computer had become an important part of the country's defense strategy.

She had enjoyed her work at the Harvard Computation Laboratory. For her civilian job she became a research fellow there. When friends asked why she didn't return to Vassar to teach, she answered simply, "Computers are more fun."

She worked with Mark II until she moved on to Mark III. This computer performed fifty times faster than Mark II because the new machine picked up instructions from reels of magnetic tape, much like those used in present-day reel-to-reel tape recorders. With Mark III, Grace created tables and graphs for scientists who did not work easily with calculus, trigonometry, and other high-level math.

But Grace was not satisfied. She wanted to teach scientists to use the computer themselves instead of depending on computer specialists. She even dreamed of a time when non-researchers would appreciate working with computers.

Grace had taken part in the development of computers ever since her first years with Mark I. Now, like a proud mother, she wanted to take her "baby" out into the world. She wanted to write computer programs that would allow factory workers, businesspeople, and salespeople to use computers.

"That can't be done," her laboratory colleagues told her. They said that only scientists had the necessary interest and skills to use computers. Who else would understand the codes? Who else would take the time to write codes in machine language? But once Grace had an idea, she wouldn't let go. She simply would not give up her vision of bringing computers to more people.

Her persistence did not pay off right away. Harvard's laboratory officials just weren't interested. Her colleagues became irritated with her for pushing so hard. Maybe that's when people began calling her feisty.

Grace was ready for a change. "I always had a queer feeling that you shouldn't take a job unless you can learn and grow in that job," she said. She discovered a chance to learn and grow with a company that built and sold computers to businesspeople. In 1949 she left Harvard to become senior programmer at Eckert-Mauchley Computer Corporation in Philadelphia, Pennsylvania.

One of Eckert-Mauchley's goals was to create a revolution in the computer industry. They planned to build the Universal Automatic Computer, UNIVAC I. This machine would be the smallest computer ever built, only about fourteen feet long and eight feet high.

It would use vacuum tubes instead of electromechanical relay switches, and it was expected to process three thousand additions in a second, twenty times faster than Mark III. Another advance was that

UNIVAC I would have internal memory. Operators could store program instructions inside the computer instead of on cards or tape.

Many computer specialists thought that simply wasn't possible. Others didn't care if it was; they were familiar with relay-switch machines and saw no reason to learn a new system. Besides, what if the plan failed? Grace had a quick answer: "It's much more fun to stick your neck out and take chances."

Grace made jokes about the possibilities of failure. "We used to say that if UNIVAC I didn't work, we were going to throw it out one side of the factory, which was a junkyard, and we were going to jump out the other side, which was a cemetery."

Even while joking, she was aware that the use of glass tubes in UNIVAC I opened up new problems in computer hardware. The five thousand tubes were easily breakable. They required tremendous amounts of energy to allow current to flow from one to the next. They could burn out, and it was difficult to have all five thousand working at the same time. To add to this problem, there was no efficient way to locate the tubes that had burned out.

The first task in building the new machine was to hire new workers. Hiring was part of Grace's job. She couldn't hire people who already knew how to program computers because there were so few programmers in the country. She had to figure out which people might be good at it. She made up a set of interview questions to find out if applicants were curious. One question was "Do you like to do crossword puzzles?" Another was "Do you like to figure out mysteries when you go to a movie or read a book?" If applicants answered yes to questions like these, there was a good chance that she would hire them. She believed that smart, curious people would enjoy computer programming. Jim McGarvey, a programmer Grace hired, said, "Nobody could fool Dr. Hopper about personality."

Although many women had stopped working outside the home after the war, Grace found and hired female applicants. "Women turn out to be very good programmers for one very good reason," she explained. "They tend to finish up things, and men don't very often finish." She believed this was because of the way girls were brought up in her day. "You don't half-cook a dinner, you finish it and put it on the table. You put the snaps and buttons on a dress. We're sort of used to finishing things." Her original staff included four men and four women.

Part of her team's job was to help workers at the Northrop Aircraft Corporation in California. They were working on a secret government contract to make missiles. Grace's team taught factory workers how to use computers to speed their work. She thought of the Harvard researchers who had said that only scientists could use computers. The researchers were wrong!

Grace taught workers to count in "computer arithmetic"—binary code. But the long strings of 0's and 1's that binary code uses could make a programmer's head spin. So sometimes programmers wrote a program in octal code, using digits 0–7, an easier code to work with. A computer could automatically translate this code into binary.

Grace was so busy teaching computer math that she had a math problem at home. "My checkbook didn't balance! It stayed out of balance for three months until I got hold of my brother, who's a banker. After several evenings of work, he informed me that at intervals, I had subtracted in octal."

Her work with UNIVAC I was more successful than her experience with her checkbook. By 1951, UNIVAC I was working! Grace and her fellow workers didn't have to use either the junkyard or the cemetery. At a party to celebrate the completion, Grace drew a cartoon with illustrations of her fellow workers and the computer. She poked fun at their struggles at the same time that she admitted her satisfaction with a difficult job well done.

Although many considered UNIVAC I a success, Grace still considered it a challenge. She wanted to see if she could make UNIVAC I help with translating its own program codes. It seemed that translat-

DECImal 10 digits	Octal 8 digits	Binary 2 digits
0	0	0
1	1	1
2	2	10
3	3	11
4	4	100
5	5	101
6	6	110
7	7	111
8	10	1000
9	11	1001
10	12	1010
11	13	1011
12	14	1100
13	15	1101
14	16	1110
15	17	1111
16	20	10000
17	21	10001
18	22	10010
19	23	10011
20	24	10100

$$
\begin{array}{r}
42 \\
+36 \\
\hline
78
\end{array}
\qquad
\begin{array}{r}
52 \\
+44 \\
\hline
116
\end{array}
\qquad
\begin{array}{r}
101010 \\
+100100 \\
\hline
100110
\end{array}
$$

ERASER

ing codes was a perfect job for a machine because the machine could never become tired or bored.

Could she program UNIVAC I to accept mathematical formulas and perform them without giving it step-by-step directions each time? Could it handle a subroutine, a group of instructions that could be coded once and called up many times? Subroutines might be the key to translating mathematical formulas. For example, an ADD subroutine might be designed that would add two numbers and store the answer in a given location. Later, the computer could "pick up" the answer and continue with further steps of the program. The computer would translate the ADD subroutine into three instructions in binary code:

- Get the first number from the specified memory location.
- Get the second number and add it to the first.
- Store the answer in a third memory location.

Grace imagined a kind of computer coding that would let a person write "$C = A + B$" and translate this into a call on the ADD subroutine: "ADD A B C." This kind of language would permit scientists and engineers to write their own computer programs. This was the centerpiece of Grace's contribution to computer programming: She moved from numerical codes to symbolic codes.

Grace envisioned a program that would be called a "compiler" today. She described her plan, borrowing an idea from libraries. Each library book bears a special code known as a call number. A person uses that code to locate a book. Grace would give each of her subroutines a special code. Her invention was a program that would read those codes and call up her subroutines. "We could start writing mathematical equations and let the computer do the work. The computer would call the pieces and put them together," she explained.

Her colleagues told her that a computer could not translate codes and call on subroutines by itself. Grace shook her head. "There stood a gadget whose whole purpose was to copy things accurately and do

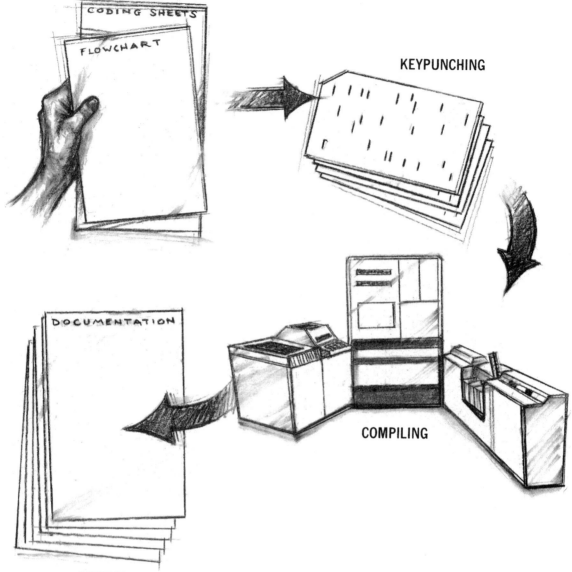

FLOWCHARTING & CODING

CODING SHEETS

FLOWCHART

KEYPUNCHING

DOCUMENTATION

COMPILING

OUTPUT

addition. And it therefore seemed sensible, instead of having programmers copy the subroutines, to have the computer copy the subroutines." Of course, this meant that the computer would need to recognize codes in one language and translate them into a series of subroutine calls.

She asked department heads if she could use their labs and workers to try out her idea. "No, you can't do that," answered one manager after another. She explained why her idea was important, but they still refused. She argued, and they called her feisty. But she kept explaining and arguing until she got space and workers to develop her compiler.

In 1952 she was ready to show her system, called the A-0 compiler, to the people who had said it couldn't be done. She prepared charts, a coding plan, and a line-by-line description of the procedure. After they watched her presentation, her audience realized that it could be done.

Because of her success with UNIVAC I, Grace got a job as Systems Engineer, Director of Automatic Programming for Remington Rand, a newly formed computer company. That same year, 1952, she was promoted to lieutenant commander in the Navy. More and more frequently, people referred to her as "Amazing Grace." Both in the computer world and in military circles, people recognized the short hair, crisp uniform, and bright-blue eyes behind steel-rimmed glasses.

Grace had not forgotten her goal of bringing computers to businesses. What good were fast and efficient programs if people wouldn't use them? "We found that we had to change from being research and development people and turn ourselves into salesmen." She "sold" her ideas to Army research departments, to the Bureau of the Census, and to New York University.

Businesspeople resisted working with computers. Grace finally figured out that they resisted because they did not use mathematical terms such as logarithm, sine, and cosine. Businesspeople worked with words like inventory (list of goods and materials), assets (items of value), and cash flow (record of moneys received and spent).

CHAPTER 6

"The Saddest Day of My Life"

With her usual energy, Grace tackled the problem of creating programs to fit business needs. This project was different from creating a language to teach the computer to work on a given formula. Now she had to include instructions such as compare and transfer.

She worked on an inventory program, a tool that would help businesses to keep records of all the items they had for sale. A business takes an inventory by recording and then counting items. Grace said she could program both these procedures. For each step of the program, she would create language to direct the computer to open and close switches, following a procedure punched into tapes.

"I was promptly told that I could not do that," Grace wrote. Just as promptly, she decided that she could.

She believed that she could design a symbolic language with which to describe business-oriented tasks. Then she could write a "compiler" program to translate that language into machine code to be "read" by the computer. By January 1955 she had completed a code with twenty commands using business words such as count and display.

Grace called her first symbolic language the A series and her second one the B series. These names made sense to her, but she was told that they were not appropriate. "It was those doggone salespeople that wanted a fancier name," she explained, "and named them such things as MATH-MATIC and ARITH-MATIC and FLOW-MATIC. You can't do anything about the sales department. You just have to let 'em go ahead." The salespeople went ahead. B series became FLOW-MATIC, and both the symbolic language and the compiler were accepted in the business world.

Salespeople at the Metropolitan Life Insurance Company used graphs translated from compiler programs to determine policy costs. The Wright-Patterson Air Force Base and Canada's Ontario Hydro used computers to record and store information.

Computers became better known and understood. Business-people asked for programs. An insurance salesperson wanted a program to compare payments and costs. A store manager wanted a program to keep track of ordering. A restaurant owner wanted a program to calculate costs of buying, cooking, and serving food.

Other programmers followed Grace's lead. By 1959 they had written many programs based on codes like Grace's instead of on numerals. Computers were becoming more user-friendly. Programmers saw a need for a common computer language, one that would allow them to share their work with each other.

A committee of computer experts met this challenge by creating COBOL, **CO**mmon **B**usiness **O**riented **L**anguage. COBOL users write formulas with characters such as plus and minus signs and command words such as MOVE and COPY. The computer translates these formulas and commands into machine language instructions.

Grace did not work directly on the development of COBOL, but she was an advisor to a subcommittee. Since her FLOW-MATIC was a model for this new language, she has been called the Grandmother of COBOL.

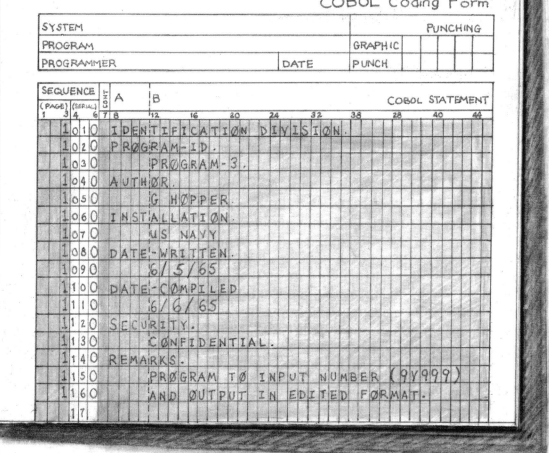

COBOL Coding Form

SYSTEM				PUNCHING				
PROGRAM			GRAPHIC					
PROGRAMMER		DATE	PUNCH					

SEQUENCE		CONT	A	B							COBOL STATEMENT		
(PAGE) 1 3	(SERIAL) 4 6	7	8	12	16	20	24	32	38	28	40	44
1 0 1	0		IDENTIFICATION DIVISION.									
1 0 2	0		PROGRAM-ID.									
1 0 3	0		PROGRAM-3.									
1 0 4	0		AUTHOR.									
1 0 5	0		G HOPPER.									
1 0 6	0		INSTALLATION.									
1 0 7	0		US NAVY									
1 0 8	0		DATE-WRITTEN.									
1 0 9	0		6/ 5/ 65									
1 1 0	0		DATE-COMPILED									
1 1 1	0		6/ 6/ 65									
1 1 2	0		SECURITY.									
1 1 3	0		CONFIDENTIAL.									
1 1 4	0		REMARKS.									
1 1 5	0		PROGRAM TO INPUT NUMBER (9Y999)									
1 1 6	0		AND OUTPUT IN EDITED FORMAT.									
1 7												

Much had happened in the sixteen years since Grace first laid eyes on the five-ton Mark I. Computers were much smaller and faster, and they were easier to operate. All over the country, people were becoming familiar with the big names in the computer industry—Remington, International Business Machines (IBM), Sperry, Rand.

Grace and her fellow programmers and computer experts congratulated themselves on the incredible success of the computer industry. They planned their future. Their goal would be to fine-tune the discoveries of the past twenty years.

The development of transistors in the early 1960s changed that goal. Transistors are devices that increase the speed and efficiency of the flow of electrical current. In computers transistors replaced vacuum tubes. They were smaller, much more reliable, used much less electricity, and did not produce so much heat. Programmers and op-

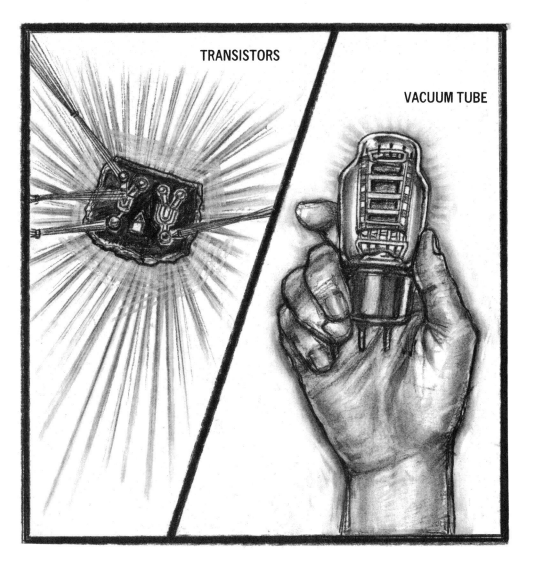

erators now concentrated on working with this technology, which made other computers old-fashioned.

Though her work life was thrilling, Grace's Navy life had its ups and downs. In 1966 she was promoted to commander. But that same year Navy officials informed Grace that she had served three years beyond the twenty-year limit for reservists. She could no longer serve.

"It was the saddest day of my life," Grace said of December 31, 1966, the day she retired.

Grace barely had time to be sad. Seven months later the Navy officials changed their minds. They were having trouble using COBOL, and they could not find anyone to solve their problems. So they decided they needed Grace after all, even though she had served too long. They asked her to serve on temporary duty for six months. "I came running—I always do when the Navy sends for me," she said.

The Navy's COBOL problem occurred because programmers and operators had created their own programming codes to solve particular problems as they arose. The new codes were fine as long as the same programmers worked on the same jobs. But when they wanted to work on another job or to share their material, they faced a computer language problem. Grace's job was to design a language that combined all the different versions of COBOL into one language, USA Standard COBOL.

She took a leave from her job at Remington Rand. Sixty-one-year-old Grace became Director of the Navy Programming Languages Group. She probably knew that some workers there gave her a less formal title—"a little old lady who talks to computers."

Later, she told interviewers that she was shocked when she first saw her office in the Pentagon, a government building in Arlington, Virginia. It was empty except for some long, detailed forms she had to fill out to get desks, chairs, file cabinets, and other supplies. Grace was ready to work, not to waste time filling out forms. She told her staff to find the materials they needed. She explained her system: "If you need something, 'liberate' or borrow it from the Air Force.... If

you can't find it from there, get it from the Army. They have almost everything, and they don't know how to count."

Nobody is sure who added the finishing touch to the office. It was a pirate's symbol—a skull-and-crossbones flag.

Her wall clock startled visitors at first. The numerals ran backward—the 11 was where they expected to see a 1, the 10 was where they expected a 2, and so on. The hands ran backward too. Grace bragged about the clock: "That's so nobody in the office can ever say 'We've always done it this way.' It tells perfectly good time. The first day people have trouble reading it. By the third day, they realize there is no real reason for the clock to run clockwise."

She thought Pentagon rules and regulations were silly, and she let everybody know that she did. She kept a child's red wagon in her office. When she wanted to send papers from her office to another office, she piled them into the wagon, added a sign that said "Classified," and pulled it along the halls.

Grace spoke simply and directly, and she worked best with others who did the same. "I am an extremely annoying employee because I won't do anything until I understand it," she admitted.

She loved to tell about not understanding a report from engineers. They described a circuit that acted in nanoseconds—billionths of a second. She wondered how far electricity could travel in a billionth of a second. She wanted to see a piece of wire that would show her how far. She called the engineers. "Please cut off a nanosecond and send it over to me."

The engineers sent her a piece of wire 11.8 inches long. "Boy, I was happy with my nanosecond," Grace told audiences. "I looked at it from all angles. I thought about it very seriously. I looked at wall switches and counted the distance to various lights." To share her delightful "discovery," she gave out 11.8-inch pieces of wire whenever she talked about nanoseconds. She had another gimmick to illustrate a picosecond—one-trillionth of a second. "Go to a fast-food restaurant," she told her audiences, "and you'll get a packet of picoseconds there. They're labeled pepper."

Grace was an eager student. Not all the people she worked with shared this trait. When she introduced a standardized COBOL program, Grace had to ask programmers to change some of their methods. Over and over she heard, "But we've always done it this way."

"I'm going to shoot somebody for saying that some day," Grace warned. "In the computer industry, with changes coming as fast as they do, you just can't afford to have people saying that."

A striking change in the computer industry started with a few grains of sand. Researchers discovered that they could make computer chips with silicon, a basic ingredient of sand. They could imbed a layer of circuits in a silicon crystal hardly thicker than the page of a book. Many electronic components such as transistors and capacitors were combined into one complex pattern called an integrated circuit. These circuits were smaller and faster than the old hand-assembled circuits made from individual transistors.

Researchers experimented until they developed an integrated circuit less than one-quarter inch square. They called it a chip. Chips could be manufactured cheaply and made it possible for small busi-

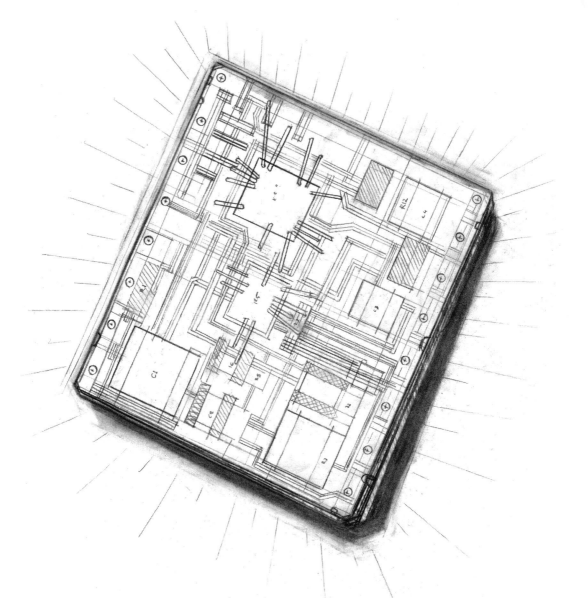

nesses to own computers. The incredible power of this microchip created new frontiers in computer development. Excited, Grace declared, "It's hard to believe that what used to be in a big blue box can all be on one chip."

Of course, Grace wanted to be in the forefront of this new development. She was delighted to receive official papers that changed her Navy assignment from a six-month temporary tour to "indefinite." She was too busy to ask what "indefinite" meant.

Over the next twenty years, Grace did a lot of consulting, lecturing, and teaching for the Navy. She was a popular speaker with plenty of facts at her fingertips as well as common sense and good humor. Businesspeople, government officials, and educators asked her to speak to their groups.

Sometimes organizations paid her well for her talks. Rita Yavinsky, who helped Grace to schedule them, revealed that Grace donated every cent of her fees to the Navy Relief Fund, money set aside for sailors and their families in need.

Whether she spoke to civilian or military audiences, Grace wore her uniform. Since few women were in the Navy, a lot of people didn't recognize the outfit. Sometimes she was mistaken for a pilot, other times for a guard.

Grace told an interviewer for TV's *60 Minutes*: "I go wandering around airports, and people come up to me and say, 'When's the next plane leave for Houston?' I got totally demoted one night in San Francisco. I got off an elevator and I heard a woman say to her husband, 'What was that?' And he said, 'That was a security guard.'"

Another story she liked to tell was about an immigration officer who asked, "What are you?" She replied, "United States Navy." He looked at her again and said, "You must be the oldest one they've got."

In her talks Grace encouraged listeners to be open to change. She reminded them that in the early 1900s people used to yell "Get a horse!" when they saw a motorist with a car problem. Now some people yelled, "Get a pencil and paper!" when they saw a computer operator with a problem. Give them time, Grace advised. "We [in computers] are now at the very beginning of what will be the largest industry in the United States."

She ended all her talks with the same two sentences: "I have received many awards and many honors. But I have already received the highest award I will ever receive—the privilege and the responsibility of serving in the United States Navy."

CHAPTER 7

Sail Out to Sea

In 1985, at the age of seventy-eight, Grace became a rear admiral. She told friends to watch the grave of her great-grandfather Admiral Russell. "He may rise from the dead," she joked.

Finally the Navy's regulations on age caught up with her. Not even Rear Admiral Grace Murray Hopper could beat them this time. In 1986, seventy-nine-year-old Grace retired again from the Navy, this time for good. Her list of awards and honorary degrees filled eight single-spaced pages. As usual she was modest: "I never thought about what I wanted to accomplish in life. I had too many things to do."

The Navy honored her request to hold the retirement ceremony on the deck of the USS *Constitution* in Boston Harbor. This ship was the oldest commissioned ship in the Navy. "We belong together," Grace joked. "After all, I'm the oldest sailor in the Navy."

She left more than memories of herself in her Pentagon office. She also left the clock that ran backward. "I gave it to the new head," she explained. "I told him he'd probably need it."

A month after she retired from the Navy, Grace became a senior consultant for Digital Equipment Corporation. "I don't think I will ever be able to really retire," she said. "I've always liked to work with either my head or my hands. I'm not content being a spectator."

Digital Equipment Corporation assigned her to represent the company in contacts with other businesses and with schools and colleges. Grace promised to work hard with students. "I'll try to push them into the future," she promised. And she did. In speeches and interviews, she frequently said, "Everybody is playing it safe. We've lost our guts.... A ship in port is safe. But that's not what ships are for. Be good ships. Sail out to sea, and do new things." She encouraged teachers and employers to give young people a chance. "People in a way are very much waiting for someone to express confidence in them," she said. "Once you do it, they'll take off."

She was asked about the role of women in the military. "As far as I'm concerned," she answered, "for women, the Navy world is best. In the Navy I had the same opportunities in training and promotions as the men—and that wasn't always true in the academic or business worlds."

She had more requests to speak than she could handle, sometimes four or five a week. She prepared outlines on about fifty different topics so she would be ready to meet any group. She could "cut a little here, a little there, add, make a new speech." She wore a symbol of her speech-making on her charm bracelet—a tiny pair of scissors.

Even in "retirement," Grace collected awards. President George Bush awarded her the National Medal of Technology. Grace was the first woman to receive this award. She loved to tell about the dinner given in her honor after the awards ceremony. When she looked at her plate, she saw flowers on her lettuce! She hesitated to eat the nasturtium salad. Then she made a quick decision. "I had to eat it. I was sitting beside the President."

Grace continued to speak and teach throughout the late 1980s, even when she walked more comfortably with a cane than without one.

After a period of poor health, Grace died in her sleep on January 1, 1992, at the age of eighty-five. As she had requested, she was buried at Arlington National Cemetery, Virginia, with a full Navy funeral. Her body was brought to the grave site in a horse-drawn, flag-draped military ammunition wagon. An honor guard played "Taps."

Honors came to Grace even after her death. In 1994 she was inducted into the National Women's Hall of Fame. The Navy announced that a guided missile destroyer would be named the USS *Hopper*.

Grace Hopper—admiral, programming pioneer, teacher, and inventor—lives on in the memories of those who worked with her. The life and work of Grace Hopper affect millions of people all over the world who accept computers as part of their everyday lives.

= 0.   434   294   481   903   251   827   651
= 2.   302   595   092   994   045   684   017

= 1. 77245 38509 05516   log √π = 0.24857   49363
  9. 86960 44010 89359   99429   97454
  0. 56418 95835   5142   50637
  0. 31830 98867   85   01273
     47756 28644 80794

  2. 50662 827   342
  0. 39894 2   658
  0. 79788   615
     02845

  1. 64 872   410
  0. 60 6   590

  1. 414   78
  1. 732   274
  2. 236   022
  2. 645   0200

  1. 464
  1. 4142   = -17-46 C.K.
  1. 73203
  3. 16227

  1. 25992
  2. 15443
  4. 64158

π   3. 14   6. 26433 83279
2π =   6. 2831   -3

π/2 =   1. 570

1/2π

π²

My detective work about Grace Hopper led me to interesting people and places. I talked with dozens of people who helped me to know her as a sister, a fellow student, a teacher, a WAVE, a computer specialist, a programmer, a speaker, a workshop leader, and a nationally known figure.

I found answers to some of the questions I started with. I know that young Grace Hopper didn't know what she wanted to be when she grew up. I know that she got some of her ideas because she was always looking for better and easier ways to perform a task. She got other ideas because she wanted everybody to appreciate computers as she did.

Grace, of course, had problems. She seemed to have three ways of handling them. For some, such as getting time and money for research, she explained, argued, and begged. For others, such as working with people who resisted change, she scolded and joked. Sometimes she met a problem, such as the Navy retirement age regulation, that she couldn't solve by explaining, arguing, or joking. She accepted that situation and looked for a new challenge.

Grace may have been smarter or harder-working or luckier than a lot of people. We can't measure these qualities. We can't measure devotion to career either, and maybe this devotion contributed most to her success.

I think that Grace Hopper's idea of fun was to learn and then to teach what she had learned.

I couldn't find any mention of heroes in her adult life. I suspect that she admired those of her colleagues who were dedicated to their jobs.

Grace Hopper is a hero to me. I admire her for her willingness to learn, to teach, and to accept challenges. Knowing about her encourages me to keep my mind open to new ideas. When someone asks me to do something I have not tried before, I want to remember what Grace said: "A ship in port is safe. But that's not what ships are for. Be good ships. Sail out to sea, and do new things."

INDEX/GLOSSARY

O

octal code 41. *A counting system that uses digits 0 to 7.*

odometer 30. *A counting machine that measures the distance a car travels.*

Ontario Hydro 47

Oughtred, William 31

P

Pascal, Blaise 29, 31

patriotism 16

Pearl Harbor, attack on 23

Pentagon 50–51, 56

Phi Beta Kappa 21. A national honorary society for students who earn top grades.

physics 19. *The science of matter and energy.*

picoseconds 53. Trillionths of a second.

programs, computer 32–36, 38, 40, 43–47, 48–50, 53

punched holes on cards 31, 34–35

R

recycling 24

relay switches 32–34, 36, 40

Remington Rand 45–47, 48–50

Roaring Twenties 17

Russell, Alexander 12, 16, 27, 56

S

silicon 53. *Chemical element, the basic ingredient of sand, that is used to make computer chips.*

60 Minutes 27, 55

slide rule 31. *A counting machine made of interconnected rulers printed with mathematical tables.*

Smith College 27–28

spectroscope 19. *An instrument that breaks light into all its different colors.*

Sperry 48

Structiron kit 10, 19

subroutines 43–44. *A group of instructions that can be coded once and called up many times.*

surveying 13–14. *A branch of applied mathematics that measures the surface of a piece of land.*

symbolic codes 43, 47

T

transistors 49–50, 53. *Devices that increase the speed and efficiency of the flow of electrical current.*

U

UNIVAC I 38, 40–41, 43, 45

USA Standard COBOL 50, 53

V

vacuum tubes 38, 40

Van Horne, John (grandfather) 13–14

Vassar College 18–19, 21–23, 27, 37

Victory Gardens 24

W

WAVES 26–27, 37, 60

weapons technology 32

weaving 31

Wilson, Woodrow 16

women, roles of 9, 16, 22, 24, 40–41, 58

World War I 15–16

World War II 23–24, 27–28, 32, 37

Wright-Patterson Air Force Base 47

Y

Yale University 21, 23

Yavinsky, Rita 55

FURTHER READING

Because the field of computers is growing so rapidly, you'll probably wind up learning most of what you want to know about these amazing machines by sitting in front of a keyboard and a monitor. But the right book can help make the picture so much clearer. And for those of you who are interested in how computers developed, there is some additional worthwhile reading.

All About Computers by Jean Atelsek
(Emeryville, CA: Ziff-Davis Press, 1993.) An attractive, solid introduction to computers for middle-grade readers, full of instructions and activities to try at home or in the classroom.

The History of Computers by Les Freed
(Emeryville, CA: Ziff-Davis Press, 1995.) Although this was intended for an adult audience, it can be enjoyed by kids because it is simply written and well-illustrated.

Internet for Kids by Deneen Frazier with Dr. Barbara Kurshan and Dr. Sara Armstrong
(Alameda, CA: Sybex, 1995.) A hot new title about a hot new area of computing. Hours of fun learning on line with this book as your guide.

The Way Things Work by David Macaulay
(Boston: Houghton Mifflin, 1988.) With more than twenty-five pages devoted to computers, including great illustrations, this is perfect for visual learners. Also has some historical material about early counting machines.

A Special Note:
IDG Books in San Mateo, California, publishes the number-one series of computer learning books for the general adult audience, with such titles as *Windows for Dummies, WordPerfect for Dummies,* and so on. Since kids are often more computer savvy than grown-ups, you may find that you're no dummy for picking up one of these books. With clear, simple language and lots of examples, they are good bets for getting you where you want to go.